ON THE WINGS OF A BUTTERFLY

A special story to support conversations on grief and loss.

Written by Belinda Messer
Illustrated by Jessica Smith

Think sweet one,
for just a minute...

...that life is like
many special moments
tied together
on a piece of string.

No one knows
how many moments
their piece of string
will hold.

For some people,
life's special moments
will be for more than a
whopping 100 years.

And for others,
life is for a shorter while.

When somebody dies,
it is only their body
that leaves us.

For every single time
that we think of them,
they will be there.
In our minds
and in our hearts,
they will live on forever.
Safe and warm
inside of us,
through our memories.

There are lots of ways
that we will remember them.
A song on the radio,
or the smell of a flower.

Maybe a delicate white feather will float down from the sky and we will remember them.

Or a big fluffy love heart
will appear in the clouds above us,
we will remember them
then too.

For some,
it's on the wings of a butterfly
that they are there.

Sometimes little babies
are born sleeping.
And the extra special
moments they live
are inside of a tummy.

The sadness that is felt
is the same
as if they had lived
a very long life.

It is ok to feel sad or angry if someone you love dies.

It is ok to cry
if someone you love dies.
Even grown ups cry.

It is ok to not understand the reasons your special one might have passed away.

Sometimes it can make you feel better if you talk about them with somebody.

Your special one doesn't want you to be sad forever. They want to see you smile again, and they want you to be happy.

Think just for a minute,
that life is like many
special moments tied on a
piece of string.

Your life is now.
It is up to you
to live it the best way
you know how.

Sing if you like to sing.
Dance or kick the ball.
Play with your friends,
do the things that make you happy.

Because that is what life is about,
sweet child,
doing the things that you love...

...and creating moments with the special people in your life. These memories will live in your heart forever.

Draw a picture of your special person

Write a few words about your special person